CW01095857

HE POETRY OF A MARRIAGE

Dennis B.Wilson

KULTURA PRESS
ESSEX, ENGLAND

THE POETRY OF A MARRIAGE

ISBN 978-0-9542899-7-3

First Published 2008 by
Kultura Press, Essex CO7 6RE

Printed in Great Britain for Kultura Press

THE POETRY OF A MARRIAGE

To Maisie.
I loved her to the end.

Contents
The Poetry of a Marriage
Poems by Dennis B. Wilson

Courtship

Fulfilment

Courtship

Maisie

To walk along the river's bank
With you, was to rejoice
In the quietly singing waters,
And the music of your voice:
In the splendour of the heavens
That reflected from your eyes:
In your hair, swept backwards on the wind,
As taken by surprise.

I held you in my eager arms,
Enchanted: gazed a while
On the rival to the moonlight
In the radiance of your smile.
It would be vain to seek excuse
For what I then must do:
The roughest wind may kiss your lips;
And so I kissed them, too.

I doubt not, through the years to come,
The skies will often shine;
And I may gaze in other eyes:
Though none so bright as thine;
But ever, as I yearn for you,
My thoughts will find you there;
With your eyes ashine with starlight,
And the wind upon your hair.

Awakening To Love

Though eyes may true and steadfast shine
Beneath a graceful brow;
Such eyes had never gazed in mine,
Until now.

The female form may waken fire,
With passion may endow;
I never felt such sweet desire,
Until now.

And kiss may hint of joyous Spring
And blossom-laden bough;
But none have caused my heart to sing,
Until now.

Though life and love are closely tied:
Synonymous; I vow
My life, of love, had been denied,
Until now.

Lonely Journey

I gazed this morning, from the lumb'ring train
That carried me, impatient, to thy side,
Upon a world obscured by drapes of rain;
Yet had the sun appeared, and swiftly dried
Those lustrous tears; and nature ev'rywhere
Had gloried in a fresh and sparkling dress;
The countryside could not have seemed more fair,
Nor heart have sung with greater happiness.

But now those treasured hours with you are past,
And I return; although the sun does smile
On joyous fields, my soul is too downcast,
And lonely yearning taints each passing mile.
That ecstasy of joy the heart conceals,
Not always wakes to shining skies above:
No song could drown the clatter of the wheels
That bear me, ever further, from My Love.

Reason For Living

The moment when you've passed from view
And left my empty heart,
The comfort of your presence fades
And hungry yearnings start;
To hold you in my loving arms
And joy in your embrace,
And lovingly and tenderly
Caress your lovely face;
To feel your body close to mine
And kiss your willing lips,
And lose the stress and worldly cares
Your soothing charms eclipse.
My life is dull and purposeless
Until you next arrive,
But when again you're in my arms
It's then I come alive.

Total Devotion

My love for you is not complex
Or hard to analyse,
It started with the little things;
The sparkle in your eyes;
Your hair in flowing, carefree waves,
That never fail to charm;
Your skin, so pale and satin-smooth;
The coolness of your arm:
Those dimples, and bewitching ears;
Your soothing fingertips;
The smile, you sometimes try to hide,
That plays around your lips:
Expressions on your changing face
That move my heart so much;
Your figure, so desirable
I scarcely dare to touch.....

And then there were the greater things;
Your gentle thoughtfulness,
Your interest and love for life,
Your feeling for distress;
The character that marks your face
With understanding rare;
Which courage, mischief, humour
And determination share.

But with your qualities, I love
Your faults, (you have a few);
Because I love the ev'rything
That totals up to – you.

The Quarrel

This day is ours,
To waste or use at will;
To make it serve our purpose well, and fill
Each fleeting moment with some worthy task
Of common usefulness: or bask
In life, and love, and mirthful happiness,
From dawn until the cloak of dusk shall close
Around the sleeping rose.

This day is short:
We have no time to fret
Away on petty quarrels, vain regret
For words far better left unsaid. Forget
The wretched past, lest otherwise it mar
The unawaiting present: lest it bar
The promise of the future.

Day will pass;
And in the cooling eve
It is not meet to think that we should leave
That harsh word unforgiven; or to grieve
For wasted hours we could have better spent
Together. Nor should we rest content
To make amends tomorrow: let us vow
For tolerance and understanding now.
To wait for time to heal the breach were vain:
Waste not this day; it will not dawn again.

To My Lady

How often I, with weary heart,
Have climbed some lonely hill
And suddenly have reached the top,
With all the world so still,
It seemed as though to even breathe
Were sacrilege indeed;
And there have gazed, and found that peace
Of which my soul had need.

And I have known the sweet release
Of cooling balm to pain;
Have half forgotten memories
And found them once again;
Have seen the angry rain-clouds flee
The laughing Summer skies;
And I have seen all these at once
Within my lady's eyes,

To feel my soul awaking
To the thrills her glances start,
Full willingly I'd give my Love,
For what it's worth, my heart.
In dismal slum; in gloomy pit;
'Mid acrid desert miles;
The loveliness of all the World
Is there, when Maisie smiles.

Natural Affinity

Of all the objects round my life,
Inanimate and dead;
I love and cherish only one:
My softly clinging bed.

And as for humans round my life,
Who number quite a host;
T'is thee my sweet, my dearest one,
I love and worship most.

From thence is but a little step
To what has crossed my mind;
What happiness! What perfect bliss!
With both my loves combin'd!

Fulfilment

Priorities

Be my Spouse.
Mind not if sometimes we neglect our home;
Leave dust in corners, smears on window glass
Or, in our garden, leave the weeds to roam
In ill-kept beds or rank, untended grass;
But love me.

Console me when I'm sad, or when I fail
And, when I'm low, my beaten spirits raise;
Restore my faith when adverse Fates prevail
And, when I earn it, let me hear your praise;
And love me.

Do not fret
If timbers rot, or ancient paint should peel,
Or cracks appear in ceilings turning grey;
But, when I need, espouse my cause with zeal:
Be loyal to me, despite what others say;
And love me.

Worry not
If shirts be less than white; or meals should burn,
And serving times be more of chance than trust;
Or buttons fall again or tears return.
Be cavalier in spending, if you must;
But love me.

Encourage my ambitions with belief,
And help me bring to life the dreams we share;
From fears and tension give me sweet relief
And, when I'm ailing, show me that you care;
And love me.

Recipe For Married Bliss

Love alone is not enough,
With it there must be
Perfect understanding,
Tact and sympathy.

Love should be unselfish,
Ruling passion's fire:
Never be possessive,
Even in desire.

Sense of humour, perfect trust,
Patient urge to please;
Tolerance and thoughtfulness:
Love will grow with these.

All these qualities will breed
Married happiness:
Love, being fed and based on each,
Cannot thrive on less.

Enduring Love

Love is like an evergreen,
That yearly stronger grew
Through calm and storm, and rain and sun;
And always sweet and new.

Passion is a fiery rose
That bloomed in Summertide
One glorious, ecstatic hour;
Then faded fast, and died.

Love is steady, calm and slow;
Passion wild and fast:
Love endures as long as life;
Passion cannot last.

Best is that relationship
Where each in turn may reign;
In which, when passion's fire is spent,
True love will still remain.

Words and Actions

When toil, want, or grief
Make a difficult road,
There are those who will join in the weeping;
But the one who takes action to lighten the load
Is the friend who is really worth keeping.

There are those who stay mute,
Or but mildly protest,
When they hear a friend unjustly slighted;
But the man worth his salt is the one who can't rest
'Till he knows that the wrong has been righted.

While a 'thank you' in words
Is a courtesy due,
And no more if repeated or shouted;
Yet a simple return by a service or two
Offers thanks that can never be doubted.

There is love that is told,
And there's love that is shown,
As from deep in the heart it comes welling;
But worthless is love that is told but not shown;
While love that is shown needs no telling.

The Seasons of Love
(The words of a song)

No flow'r can bloom for ever, Dear, but nature, to atone,
Gives ev'ry season through the year a beauty of its own.
Life also has its seasons clear, with each a beauty rare;
And the seasons of life can be seasons of love,
With one like you to share.

In Springtime the golden daffodils awoke to greet the sun;
And in ourselves the tender bloom of love
made two hearts beat as one.
When in June the rose burst forth,
to glory in the heat of Summer's fire,
Our love burn'd fierce with impatient youth,
and eagerness to meet desire.

But just as those tender leaves of green mature to Autumn red;
With love grown strong through years of toil and care,
serene, we gaze ahead.
All too soon the Winter trees
will show their branches stark against the sky;
Tho' flow'rs may wither: the earth grow cold:
my love for you will never die.

Disillusionment

Profit and Loss

I met a lovely, loving lass,
And she became my wife;
And children then, to mark our love,
Was all I asked of life.

I had a lovely baby girl,
I had a loving wife;
I only needed then a son,
To make complete my life.

I had a daughter, wife and son,
And all I asked of life;
But then she gave them all her love
And ceased to be a wife.

Change of Life

She was proud, once, to be her own person,
With a quirkiness hard to resist;
And she freely gave way to emotions
To be hugged, and be fondled, and kiss'd.
She employed, and enjoyed, sexual freedom.
(Even slightly, delightfully, lewd);
But she's now just a slave to convention,
And a timid and old-fashioned prude.

Thoughts on a Wedding Anniversary

There was a time, but long ago,
(And those were happy days),
When you revealed your love for me
In countless pleasant ways;
And though in dark and love-filled nights
You spoke your love as well,
Your feelings were so evident
You had no need to tell.

But now you give me only words,
And those too few and rare
To justify or earn belief,
Or prove you even care,
Without supporting evidence
However brief or small
By glance, or touch, or thoughtful act,
That love exists at all.

And even if I take your word:
My well-formed doubts disown:
What worth has love but rarely told
And never, ever shown?
For should that love you still profess
Tomorrow, unmourned, go;
What would be diff'rent? What would change?
How would I ever know?

Bitter-Half

My wife and myself were once happy indeed;
That bliss we shall never forget;
But then came the day it was all doomed to end:
You ask me what happened? We met.

My dear wife is one in a million, no less,
But no, I don't think she's a Queen;
I still say she's one in a million, (or more),
A million just like her, I mean.

I know her opinions as well as my own,
For she'll hold the opposite view:
There's nothing my wife wouldn't do for me now;
Yes, nothing is just what she'll do.

My wife will admit if she's ever at fault,
Her will, (like her won't), is so strong:
I mean that she will should occasion arise,
But she says she has never been wrong.

My wife, to be fair, thinks I've only two faults
That arouse her complaints day-by-day:
The first one encompasses all that I do,
The second is all that I say.

Anniversary Card

The sentiments the cards express
Speak well of married life;
This tells of love that never dies,
And that, "My perfect wife;"
But these apply to other pairs,
(or even us in youth):
I seek a card to mark the day,
But one that speaks the truth
Or one, at least, that does not hide
Or cultivate a sham,
(I hope I'm not a hypocrite,
Whatever else I am).
But not to cause a public hurt
I look for words that state
The day's expected message;
Not to whom they may relate.
So greetings, loved and loving wife;
All happiness to thee:
The very best in all the World,
(Whoever you may be).

Three Women

The French, who claim to know so much
In matters of the heart,
Say, "In the life of ev'ry man
Three women play a part;
The first the woman that he loved,
And loves, for all his life;
The second she who loves but him;
The third he takes to wife."

I know the woman I have loved,
I know the one I wed;
(If these were two, or two-in-one,
I'll leave for now unsaid).
There's one intriguing question left,
I wonder, who was she
Of all I've known and met through life;
The woman who loved me?

Words Can Never Hurt Me

"What have you ever done?" she demanded,
"Or accomplished, to stand in good stead?
You are nothing!" she added, with venom;
"You are nobody!" sneering, she said.
But 'nothing' can not be diminished,
So why should that cause me dismay?
And as to her other opinion
Well, 'Nobody's' perfect, they say!

Fulfilment

This life, with approval and praise for our deeds,
And with love and respect, can be sweet;
But so often by one other person, those needs
Must be given, to make joy complete.

I never sought money with wealth as my aim,
But the all that I needed I earned;
For riches can't buy the true values I'd name,
And for some of the best I have yearned.

I've known a few triumphs: that taste of success
Would be sweet 'till the end of my days;
If only I thought I had gained your respect,
And if only you gave me your praise.

I've joyed in our children, a joy that we shared,
And there's nothing I valued above;
I could truly be happy, if only you cared,
And if only you gave me your love.

Forgive and Forget

You wound with words you recklessly select
And then, without expression of regret;
Quite unaware or heedless of effect,
Assume that I'll as easily forget.
A Christian should forgive, and should forget,
The hurts of yesterday and yesteryear;
But how to put it out of mind, when yet
The memory remains so cruelly clear?
A willingness to place beyond recall
Each bitter gibe; each painful hurt or slight;
Is not itself the means to end it all,
As simply done as switching off a light.
And if you voice no sorrow or regret,
Or seek forgiveness for your verbal knives;
Although I want to pardon and forget,
The poison festers, spoiling both our lives.
Denied the chance or reason to forgive;
Unable to forget what has been said;
The soul corrodes, and kindness cannot live,
And soon the small remaining love is dead.

Glimpses of the Past

I view the woman you've become
And, sadly, love is dead;
But still today, and evermore,
I love the girl I wed.

I hate the bitter thoughts you rouse,
That will not set me free;
But sometimes glimpse, though rarely now,
The girl you used to be.

The girl who loved me for myself,
Who caring was, and kind;
Before my failings and my faults
Came foremost in her mind.

The girl who laughed, and gave to life
A sense of joy, and fun;
Who gave me freely of her love,
So two became as one.

Then, once again, you wake my heart
Before returns, the pain;
And for that joyous, fleeting space,
I love you once again.

Ruby Wedding Anniversary

I thank you for the years of love
That made it bliss to be alive:
The years of joy and happiness
That number twenty five.

But silver's twenty-five you say:
It's ruby now? Of course I know
The day you pledged your lifelong love
Was forty years ago.

I mourn the wasted latter years;
The happiness that could have been;
The years of cold indifference;
The lost and gone fifteen.

Despair

Words on the Card

'Only you and I can know
The meaning of this day
And all the many thoughts it brings
Too dear for words to say.
We share alone its memories
That add so dear a part
To all the ties between us now
That bind us heart to heart.'
© Hallmark Cards inc.

'Only you and I can know
The meaning of this day
And all the many thoughts it brings
Too dear for words to say.'
Too dear: that is they cost too much
In wasted, loveless years;
Your secret thoughts are guilty ones;
Mine bitter ones, in tears.

'We share alone its memories
That add so dear a part
To all the ties between us now
That bind us heart to heart.'
Ties now become a stranglehold
That throttled love to death;
And spoiled the happy memories
With ev'ry dying breath.

Prisoner of Conscience

When two are joined by marriage vows
To love 'till death shall part,
They mean sincerely what they say:
They promise from the heart.

They can't foresee maturer years
When natures will have changed;
And some will ever closer grow,
But more become estranged.

The law provides a remedy
For those who can evade
The deeply sacred nature
Of the promises they made.

But some must live by Holy Writ
Man's laws can not amend;
Imprisoned by a solemn vow
That only death can end.

Unrequited Love

Stage one was when you first awoke desire,
And I became a victim of your charms;
And you responded then with equal fire:
Returned my kisses: held me in your arms.

Stage two began with habit in your touch,
And then the false excuses nightly told;
And I held back. I loved you just as much,
But knew your sole reaction would be cold.

Stage three is now, when I no longer yearn
To kiss or hold, and bitter feel instead.
Without the love it needed in return
Starvation had one end: my love is dead.

The Last Word

Her nature was to speak her hasty mind
In rage, and then forget the taunts she'd blurt;
His nature more inclined to let things pass
But fight when roused, and after, nurse each hurt.

The rows became more frequent year by year;
The words more hurtful, aimed to cause more pain,
And longer lasting; causes more absurd;
And past recriminations voiced again.

The truth of who was right and who was wrong
Could never be determined, now so blurr'd;
The issue less important than the fight;
Her major aim to have the final word.

The endless friction took its toll, and broke
His for-love-yearning, once-so-loving, heart;
First death to love, then after, death itself
Had forced the two contestants far apart.

She thought upon the lonely years ahead
Though, being alone, her sobs were never heard;
And pride gave way to guilt and late regret
That she had always had the final word.

But not the true last word: when tempers rage
The strongest love is bound to wilt and die;
And harsh and thoughtless words reduce to one:
The true last word, though never said, 'Goodbye.'

Words of Sadness

In ev'ry language words have means and pow'r
To praise, condemn, or wound, or love or hate;
But saddest are those words, in any tongue,
That tragically signify, 'Too late.'

Too late to talk to children, once so young:
To share their forming thoughts and join their play
Who, all-too-soon, are suddenly full-grown,
And gone to take their paths along life's way.

Too late to turn and make that other choice
That could have meant a more rewarding life;
Or court that other friend who might have proved
A better husband: longer-loving wife.

Too late to hear, and open now the door,
That distant knock of opportunity;
Or use those talents, promising so much,
Allowed through dire neglect to atrophy.

Too late, when death has parted those who loved
But, at the end, were scarcely even friends,
To utter words of sorrow; or forgive;
Or say, "I love you still;" or make amends.

Thoughts in the Long and Lonely Night

What made you, when I asked you, breathe, "O yes!"
What made you favour me to share your life?
I wonder, was it really me you loved,
Or did you love the thought of being a wife?
How cruel you were, if status was your aim,
To rob me of what could have been in store;
I might have known, although I loved her less,
True happiness with one who loved me more.
The love I gave to you, and you alone,
You starved and left to die from cold neglect;
I mourn throughout the sleep-denying night
What might have been, and bitterly reflect
That in your eyes I once did little wrong
But now: God knows I try! Can do no right:
Disinterest, contempt, my lot by day:
Indifference my cold reward at night.
You find no words to mark the things I do,
But endless scorn for tasks I've left undone;
No word of consolation when I fail;
No welcome praise for things achieved or won.
Each night I yearn to take you in my arms,
But know that you would spurn my tender hold;
How can a body, outwardly so warm,
Be inwardly unyielding, and so cold?
And when my passing ends your broken vow
To love and cherish, 'til death does us part;
Though tears will doubtless wet your public face,
I think no grief will touch your private heart.
Who then will make your happiness his aim,
And reap the love that once to me you swore?
I hope he may succeed where I have failed
But even so, he will not love you more.

Death

Unanswerable Question

In your final conscious moments, too exhausted then, to speak,
You awkwardly but lovingly caressed my tear-wet cheek;
And this you did repeatedly to me and, one-by-one,
The daughter that I know you loved and well-belovéd son.
And now the question tortures me, for I shall never know;
Was this the love you really felt and in the end could show
Or, wanting to express to them true love you could not tell
And, knowing they were watching you, included me as well?
I only know, each time I see those symbols of despair;
A made but ever-vacant bed, an always-empty chair,
I grieve for you but also mourn, with sad and angry tears,
The happiness we could have had in all those wasted years.

Afterlife

Old Man's Fantasy?

In the Springtime of my life
I found the ecstasy of life,
With all its alternating happiness and pain;
And I loved and left, or loved and lost,
And did not rue the cost,
Because I knew for sure that I would love again.

In the Summer of my life
I gave my love for half my life,
And I was faithful to the vows that I had made;
But what her love had been as bride
Was but a fire that slowly died,
And all those years bereft of love the price I paid.

In the Autumn of my life
I thought that never more in life
Would I feel love, and then be loved in full return;
But the heart can still desire,
And I discovered passion's fire
That for so long had smouldered, still could fiercely burn.

In the Winter of my life
Yours is the love that gives me life,
And all my love I give to you, with joy and pain;
And the perfect love you bring
Inspires my heart and soul to sing
And now, in Winter, I am living Spring again.